MW01200122

Preface

I started writing devotions about twenty years ago while I was volunteering as a Sunday school teacher for high school students. I wanted to find a way to keep the youth engaged during Holy Week, so I started sending my students daily emails. Those emails during Holy Week extended to daily devotions during Lent and Advent. Over the years, the distribution list expanded at the encouragement of my friend Becky Szeyller. Now I write weekly devotions in addition to daily devotions for Advent and Lent.

I try to see God in all that I do. Recognizing God in the simple details of life encourages me, teaches me, and often makes me laugh. Advent can be a hectic time, and before you know it, the season is over. These daily devotions may help you pause for a moment, take a breath, and see God in a new light as you make your way to the manger this Advent season.

FIRST SUNDAY OF ADVENT

Picking Raspberries

A voice of one calling: "In the desert prepare the way for the
Lord; make straight in the wilderness a highway for our God."
—Isaiah 40:3 NIV

See, I am doing a new thing! Now it springs up;
do you not perceive it? I am making a way in
the desert and streams in the wasteland.
—Isaiah 43:19 NIV

The theme for this Advent season is "A Way to the Manger." Like
everyone in the story of Jesus's birth, we each have a unique path
when it comes to finding our way to God. Some paths are long,
arduous, and uncomfortable, like that of the very pregnant Mary
riding the donkey to Bethlehem. Some are joyous, like the shepherds'
race into town after their encounter with the angels. Some are thrust
on us, as with Joseph in a time of crisis. Suffice it to say, there are a
lot of ways to the manger—a lot of ways to God—but they all end at
the same place: in His presence.

The information in the Bible surrounding Jesus's birth is very
familiar. We know about the shepherds, the wise men, the gifts,
Bethlehem, and Mary and Joseph. Those are all easy stories to pick
out. What's more interesting is discovering the parts of the story that
are hidden—like the raspberries in my raspberry bushes. I've learned
to walk through my raspberry patch at least twice each time I pick.

The first time through, I pick the berries that are obvious and easy to reach. The second time I pass through, I reach for the ones farther off the path. I kneel, sometimes on my hands and knees, pushing leaves aside, reaching through the scratching branches, and look up, under, and around to find the ripe berries. Often, it's the hidden berries that are the biggest and sweetest. It is my earnest prayer that as we go through this Advent season together, we will all discover hidden paths of the story of Jesus's birth to bring new excitement and energy into what is already an exciting and joyous event.

These devotions should get you thinking—should get you to look beyond the tangled branches of stress, to-do lists, work, worry, and all the rest and view the story of Jesus's birth from a new angle. Kneel, look up, open your eyes and heart, and listen to God. The birth of His Son, Jesus, proves that He is accessible to all and eager to be with us. Just His name, Emmanuel, which means "God with us," is a huge spoiler alert. Consider your own way to the manger this Advent, and keep your eyes focused on the goal ahead.

Dear God,
As we start this Advent season and consider our way to
the manger, help us keep our eyes open, give us flexibility
to kneel before You, and allow us to see You!

The Way

A voice of one calling: "In the desert prepare the way for the
Lord; make straight in the wilderness a highway for our God."
—Isaiah 40:3 NIV

And I will put enmity between you and the woman,
and between your offspring and hers; he will crush
your head, and you will strike his heel.
—Genesis 3:15 NRSV

The way to the manger did not start with the first few chapters of
Matthew or Luke, or even with Isaiah. The way to the manger started
in the book of Genesis. It originated in the Garden of Eden, went
through Adam and Eve's sin, stared the serpent in the face, and just
kept going.

In the beginning, the way to God was as simple as taking a walk in a
garden in the cool of the day (Genesis 3:8). God's plan was to be with
His creation, to be in relationship with us. There were no deserts,
no need to make anything straight, no wilderness—just unfettered
access to God, with no sin to get in the way. That didn't last long. Just
a few verses later, Adam and Eve decided to make their own path,
a path that, according to the serpent, would lead to wisdom. Who
among us has not thought at least once that we know better than
God? The way to the manger started because people messed up the
easy path and put down a million orange cones and detour signs.

God didn't make access to Him difficult—we did. We still do. We focus on our own plans, we don't trust God's plan, and we seek wisdom via shortcuts ("Want to be smart? Eat an apple."). Rather than spend time with God and learn wisdom that way, we try to make our own paths. Self-help books are bestsellers because people would rather read a ten-step guide to happiness than spend ten minutes reading the Bible.

The way to the manger is not a path we are intended to walk alone; we are intended to walk it with God. Satan will bite at our heels the whole way, but the One we walk with is able to crush his head. God is keenly aware that we often have the attention span of gnats and get sidetracked easily. We take our focus off Him and put it on ourselves. But He is patient. When we turn back to Him, He grabs us by the shoulders and sets us back on the path again and again. Get on your path, set your eyes on Him, and keep making your way to the manger.

Dear God,
I struggle so often with staying on the path because
there are so many things that take my attention
away from You. Please keep me focused today.

Are We There Yet?

> From Mount Hor they set out by the way to the
> Red Sea, to go around the land of Edom; but the
> people became impatient on the way.
> —Numbers 21:4 NRSV

According to the *Oxford English Dictionary*, aside from the four Sundays preceding Christmas, *advent* means "coming" or "the arrival of a notable person or thing." Of course, if someone is due to arrive, that usually means someone else is waiting for the arrival. To me, waiting is just an opportunity to be impatient. Whether it's waiting for a traffic light to change, a cake to bake, a plane to land, or as children waiting for Christmas to come, like the Israelites in the desert with Moses, we get "impatient on the way."

This verse from Numbers gives us part of the route taken by the Hebrews as they traveled to Canaan. I found a biblical map that showed the route the Hebrews took from Egypt to Canaan, and it also showed the usual caravan route from Egypt to Canaan. There is quite a difference—one is pretty direct (the caravan route), and one is not (the Moses route). You can understand why the Hebrews were impatient. They must have asked, "Are we there yet?" hundreds of times. But there was a reason that God led the Hebrews on such a circuitous route. Aside from the Hebrews' need to purge Egypt and four hundred years of slavery out of their systems, the route that God took them on also helped them avoid conflicts with some of the local people—in this verse, the Edomites.

Our way to the manger isn't always clear or straight, and it doesn't always make sense to us. Isaiah prophesied about the coming of the Messiah more than six hundred years before Jesus was born. In the interim, the Israelites were scattered and taken to foreign lands and then returned to find their temple destroyed and their land a mess. We get impatient because we don't understand the direction our path is going. We want to get from point A to point B and get there as efficiently and easily as possible, but that's not always God's way. What if your way to the manger has twists and turns because God is directing you out of harm's way? What if God is trying to teach you something or rid you of old habits? What if God is trying to get you to focus on Him—to trust *Him*—rather than on your own understanding?

During Advent, we wait for the coming of Christ. We wait to celebrate His birth again, and we wait for the day that He will return. Like the Hebrews, our paths both individually and as a group of believers have been filled with hills, valleys, twists, and turns. We are lost and found, obedient and stubborn, humble and proud, impatient and submissive. Trust in God and stay on the path He has planned for you.

Dear God,
Help me to put my trust in You as I make my way to the manger and give me patience to stay on the path.

Parker House Rolls, Part 1

On entering the house, they saw the child with Mary
his mother; and they knelt down and paid him homage.
Then, opening their treasure chests, they offered
him gifts of gold, frankincense, and myrrh.
—Matthew 2:11 NRSV

If you will only heed his every commandment that I am
commanding you today—loving the Lord your God, and
serving him with all your heart and with all your soul.
—Deuteronomy 11:13 NRSV

One of my contributions to Thanksgiving dinner was going to be homemade Parker House rolls. I settled on the recipe weeks in advance, knew that I had all the ingredients, and was eager to bring fresh-baked bread for the big family meal. I got up early Thanksgiving morning and got to work: I prepared the yeast and mixed and kneaded all the ingredients until I had a perfect little mound of bread dough. I was even thinking about the verses in the Bible that talk about yeast. (Surely if I was thinking about God, it would all turn out great!) As I was cleaning up, I realized that I'd forgotten to add the "three slightly beaten eggs" to the dough. *You have got to be kidding me!* After standing in the kitchen for a few minutes not knowing whether to laugh or cry, I decided to beat the eggs and try to incorporate them into my perfect little mound of bread dough. I made a huge mess—I had three slightly beaten eggs all over the kitchen counter! What was a beautiful, smooth mound of dough became a lumpy, mutant pile of yellow goo. There had to be a devotion in this …

What if one of the wise men had forgotten to bring his gift? What if all along the journey Wise Man 3 thought for sure he'd put his gift of myrrh in his camel saddlebag—he was sure it was there!—and then, when he and the other two wise men got to the manger and went to retrieve their gifts to give to the King of the Jews, all he had in his saddlebag was an extra pair of socks? Do you rewrite the Bible verse and say that the wise men brought gold, frankincense, and a pair of socks, when it was supposed to be myrrh? How humiliating and frustrating! Wise Man 3 came all that way, did all that preparation to offer a special gift, and blew it.

What if on your way to the manger you think you're bringing Jesus this great gift—maybe you wrote a beautiful song, painted an exquisite landscape, wrote a poem, built a crib, made Parker House rolls, or prepared something else that's an expression of your love for Him—and when you get there it's not at all what you planned? Maybe it's boring or a hot mess, or simply pales in comparison to what others have brought him. Giving God gifts and offerings is important, but what He wants is our hearts. You don't need to buy or make anything to bring with you on your way to the manger. You just need to bring your heart to Him. (Although socks might be good on a cold day.)

Dear God,
I get so frustrated when I mess up and am humiliated by my fruitless efforts. I forget that what You want is my heart.

Parker House Rolls, Part 2

On entering the house, they saw the child with Mary
his mother; and they knelt down and paid him homage.
Then, opening their treasure chests, they offered
him gifts of gold, frankincense, and myrrh.
—Matthew 2:11 NRSV

If you will only heed his every commandment that I am
commanding you today—loving the Lord your God, and
serving him with all your heart and with all your soul.
—Deuteronomy 11:13 NRSV

I know you're wondering what happened with the Parker House rolls. Well, I was afraid that the first batch was ruined, so I decided to make another batch right away. That's when I realized I didn't have enough flour, so I had to run to the nearby convenience store to get more. As I was driving there, I was thinking about my grandma, who passed away a few years ago (I often think of my grandma when I'm upset), so I had tears streaming down my face by the time I parked my car. As God would have it, I saw a friend from church who I've been with on many youth mission trips. He has seen me sweaty, dirty, and frustrated, so seeing me with my face streaked with tears and flour, the three slightly beaten eggs all over me—not to mention the fact that I hadn't showered—he was unfazed by my appearance. I gave him a quick rundown of what had happened, and we laughed at the absurdity of it all. "Lis," he said, "it's all part of the journey." In my mind, I heard, "It's all part of your way to the manger."

I bought the flour, came home, and made the second batch of dough. Both batches turned out great (apparently three slightly beaten eggs aren't as important as they think they are), and I have enough Parker House rolls for the next five holidays. If you need Parker House rolls, just come to my house. They're in the freezer!

The verse in Matthew is worth a second read because when you look at it closely, it says the wise men "paid him homage" and *then* offered their gifts of gold, frankincense, and socks—I mean myrrh. *Homage* is defined as an expression of high regard or a ceremony where one acknowledges himself to be a subordinate of a lord. The first thing we need to do on the way to the manger, or at least when we get there, is to express our high regard to the One who is the Lord of us all. We need to pay Him homage before we do anything else. If I can do that, if I can acknowledge that the child in the manger is the Lord, my Lord, then no matter what gift I bring, my heart will be in the right place and He will accept my gift gladly. Gifts and offerings are outward displays of what's in our hearts. If my heart is in the right place, my gifts and offerings to God can be as valuable as gold, frankincense, and myrrh. And, as I learned with my Parker House rolls, they can be abundant and overflowing—enough for everyone and then some!

Dear God,
I pay You homage and acknowledge that You are
my Lord. Accept my gifts and offerings and let
them be a blessing to You and to others.

Lisa M. Black

Preserving the Way

He stores up sound wisdom for the upright; he is a shield
to those who walk blamelessly, guarding the paths of
justice and preserving the way of his faithful ones.
—Proverbs 2:7–8 NRSV

But the angel said to him, "Do not be afraid, Zechariah,
for your prayer has been heard. Your wife Elizabeth
will bear you a son, and you will name him John."
—Luke 1: 13 NRSV

Zechariah and Elizabeth waited years for a child, but as they were
"both getting on in years," the prospect of a having a child was
becoming more remote. Zechariah and Elizabeth were exactly the
type of people described in Proverbs; they lived blamelessly, they
acted righteously, and they were faithful and obedient (Luke 1:6).
You'd think that people like that would have a pretty easy way to the
manger. If God was going to answer anyone's prayers, it would be
the prayers of people like Zechariah and Elizabeth—or at least that's
what we want to believe.

So much about our way to the manger is about trusting God, but
trusting God is difficult. Trusting God is even more difficult when
we are doing what He asks and our lives are still hard. There are
missionaries who are faithful to God who put their lives on the line
every day; there are poor and homeless people who are faithful to

God but are hungry and cold every day; there are people full of love who are eager to be parents and obedient to God but who remain childless. Elizabeth and Zechariah probably prayed daily for a child, and for years, the answer was no. But instead of being bitter, they remained faithful to God.

God's plan for Elizabeth and Zechariah was for them to have a child, but on His timetable. John had to be born at a certain time because he played a very important role in Jesus's life. If he had been born years earlier, John and Jesus would have had a very different relationship.

How do you prevent bitterness and frustration from taking you off the path? Zechariah and Elizabeth chose to remain obedient. God was "preserving the way" of his faithful servants even though that way was not what they were hoping for. When we're struggling on our way to the manger, maybe it would help if we remembered that God is preserving our way. Zechariah and Elizabeth probably had no idea that God was shielding, guarding, and preserving their way, but He was. I need to be cognizant of the fact that while I am certainly not blameless or always faithful, God is shielding, guarding, and preserving my way too.

Dear God,
I can't see the way You have laid out for
me, but I want to trust that You
are protecting me along the way.

DAY 7

I Love to Laugh

Then our mouth was filled with laughter, and our tongue with shouts of joy; then they said among the nations, "The Lord has done great things for them."
—Psalm 126:2 ESV

But the angel said to them, "Do not be afraid; for see—I am bringing you good news of great joy for all the people."
—Luke 2:10 NRSV

We see a lot of strange things on our way to the manger. Just the other day, I saw an inflatable lawn ornament of Darth Vader and a stormtrooper holding candy canes. I'm a huge *Star Wars* fan, but I never really considered that to be related to Christmas. A day later, I was walking downtown and noticed in a store window a mannequin dressed in holiday clothes, and it was in the oddest pose with hips thrust forward and torso leaning too far back – no one would or could stand like that. Both of those sights made me laugh out loud and reminded me that *joy* is part of this season and needs to be part of our way to the manger.

God is hilarious. I think that if God laughed, it would be one of those laughs that comes from your toes and brings tears to your eyes. I love laughing like that! I was with my family at SeaTac airport a few summers ago waiting for our red-eye flight. It was late, and we were all exhausted. My daughter, Emily, and I were watching a movie, and there was a scene that made me laugh so hard I was crying and could barely breathe. I hope you've experienced that kind of laughter—it's one of the best things ever!

There's a lot to be serious and thoughtful about during Advent, but there's a lot to be joyful about too. Our way to the manger can be very challenging: our faith wavers, our steps falter, and sometimes we just completely fall off the path. I think that's why God gives us things to laugh about. There were several strange sights on the way to the manger in Bethlehem. The star that shone over Bethlehem was so remarkable that the wise men from the east (presumably quite a distance away) had to come see it. While they probably didn't laugh at the sight of the star, their excitement and joy must have been overwhelming! The angels in the field with the shepherds was another strange sight—not ha-ha funny, more like scare the daylights out of you—but it resulted in the shepherds running into Bethlehem looking for Jesus. They could not contain their joy!

Unexpected sights on our way to the manger can bring us joy and even make us laugh out loud. The announcement of Jesus's birth was "good news of great joy for all people." During this season, play a game with the family, look for the absurd and silly, or watch a funny movie. Have a good laugh on your way to the manger!

Dear God,
You have done great things for me, and I am filled with joy!

Lisa M. Black

SECOND SUNDAY OF ADVENT
Little Town of Bethlehem

All went to their own towns to be registered. Joseph
also went from the town of Nazareth in Galilee to Judea,
to the city of David called Bethlehem, because he was
descended from the house and family of David.
—Luke 2:3–4 NRSV

But you, Bethlehem Ephrathah, though you are small among the
clans of Judah, out of you will come for me one who will be ruler
over Israel, whose origins are from of old, from ancient times.
—Micah 5:2 NIV

A certain man of Bethlehem in Judah went to live in the
country of Moab, he and his wife and two sons.
—Ruth 1:1 NRSV

Bethlehem first appears in Genesis as the burial place of Rachel, Jacob's wife, the mother of Joseph and Benjamin. Bethlehem comes up again as the place where Ruth met her second husband, Boaz, and from there, we see her role in the line of David (Ruth was David's great-grandmother). For a little town, Bethlehem featured prominently in both the Old Testament and the New Testament.

Our way to the manger has to go through Bethlehem. It is a reminder of God's fulfillment of His prophecy to Micah, it is another tie between Jesus and David, and it is God's way of letting us know that great things can come from the least obvious sources. Focusing specifically on Bethlehem on the second Sunday in Advent is kind of like looking through the wrong end of a microscope lens or through the small end of a funnel: in looking from the perspective of the small thing, we get a glimpse of the much bigger picture of Jesus's birth—its context in history and the extent of God's plan.

As we make our way to the manger and through our faith, we rarely see the results of the seeds that we plant, but if we are wise and thoughtful, we can see how those who came before us helped us to become the people we are. We are all small, like Bethlehem, but God can do great things through us. Peter was a fisherman and became the rock on which God built His church; Ruth was a widow with no real prospects for being anything other than a widow, but she was part of the line of David; Joseph was a prisoner in Egypt and rose to political heights; Bethlehem was a little town that became the birthplace of the Messiah. Our way to the manger may seem insignificant, but never underestimate God's plan for you or your impact on others!

Dear God,
I am the seed that was planted by others. Please
help me to uphold that responsibility.

Be the Light

May God be gracious to us and bless us and make his
face to shine upon us, that your way may be known
upon earth, your saving power among all nations.
—Psalm 67:1–2 NRSV

The people who walked in darkness have seen a great light; those
who lived in a land of deep darkness—on them light has shined.
—Isaiah 9:2 NRSV

Who among us has not engaged in some level of Monday-morning
quarterbacking? Once we're on the other side of a situation, we often
look back and with our twenty-twenty hindsight see what went wrong
and what went right. We see the signs we missed and think that if
we'd seen them before, the way could have been a whole lot different.
Part of our problem is that we often walk in darkness on our way to
the manger and through our faith. The darkness we walk through
can be the result of grief or anger, or simply because we choose to
not open our eyes. The book of Isaiah was full of prophecies about
the coming Messiah—he would be born in Bethlehem, to the line
of David. There were even prophecies about his death. In hindsight,
how could the people not have known that Jesus, that baby born in
Bethlehem, was the Son of God? If the prophecies weren't enough,
then the star in the sky and the angels in the field should have been
more than sufficient to shine the light on those in the dark. It all
seems so obvious now, doesn't it?

Like the book of Isaiah, the New Testament is full of prophecies about the Second Coming—how He will come in the clouds, in the twinkling of an eye—and the book of Revelation is all about the Second Coming. There is no shortage of information, or light, provided by God to illuminate our way, but like the people in Bethlehem and Judea when Jesus was born and during His ministry, we may not recognize what will seem so obvious after Jesus comes again. We all walk in a certain amount of darkness—we can't help it. We fumble around on our way to the manger wearing blindfolds that we insist on keeping tied tightly over our eyes.

We need to be people of the light—it will make it easier for us to make our way to the manger. The verse in Psalms says that when God's face shines on us, His way may be known on the earth and His saving power revealed. We are supposed to reflect the light of God's face so that other people will know Him and His saving power. As we reflect the light of God, we light the way for others to get out of the darkness. That means everyone has to do their part along the way to the manger. Offer encouragement to others, seek God's wisdom as you offer guidance to someone who is struggling, or volunteer at a soup kitchen. Get out there and reflect the light of God, because someone out there is in desperate need of it. Your way to the manger is not just about you—this is a group effort. We need each other. We need to reflect the light of God to one another so that everyone can know God's saving power.

Dear God,
Let me reflect Your light to help light the
way for others to know You!

Lisa M. Black

Benefit of the Doubt

And she gave birth to her firstborn son and wrapped
him in bands of cloth, and laid him in a manger,
because there was no place for them in the inn.
—Luke 2:7 NRSV

The Lord does not look at the things people look at. People look
at the outward appearance, but the Lord looks at the heart.
—1 Samuel 16:7 NIV

An engaging story requires some level of tension—a "good guy"
and a "bad guy" and some sort of conflict or challenge that needs to
be overcome. In the story of Jesus's birth, I've often considered the
innkeeper to be kind of a bad guy. How could he not let Joseph and
Mary stay inside the inn when Mary was clearly very, very pregnant?
That's just mean. The innkeeper is mentioned only in this one verse
in Luke, so we don't have a lot to go on, but based on this limited
impression, he doesn't seem like a very nice man.

What if we give the innkeeper the benefit of the doubt? Bethlehem
was chock-full of people for the census; there were probably hundreds
of people looking for a place to stay. The inn may have been bursting
at the seams, so much so that the innkeeper didn't have the option of
giving Mary and Joseph a room—there literally was no place for them
to sleep. Maybe offering them a place in the cave with the animals
was the only thing the innkeeper had to give them.

As we make our way to the manger and navigate our lives, we can be quick to decide who is good and who is bad based on very little information. I've judged the innkeeper for years based only on "there was no place for them in the inn." We see in 1 Samuel that God doesn't look at the things people look at—He looks at the heart. How would our way to the manger be different if we tried to look at others through a pair of "God glasses"? Quite frankly, I don't always want to have a pair of God glasses; I don't want to know that there is kindness in someone I've prejudged. I want to make a snap decision based on very little information.

God looked at Mary's heart and saw a heart that was faithful, willing, and obedient. God looked at Joseph's heart and saw one that was righteous, fearful, kind, and obedient. God looked at the hearts of the shepherds and saw ones that were open, brave, and compassionate. God looked at the hearts of the wise men and saw intelligence, commitment, and humility. God saw more in all these people than anyone else would have or could have and made them all key figures in the story of Jesus's birth. God looked at the innkeeper's heart and saw more than I did. Maybe God saw a heart that was eager to help and thought outside the box. I think I need God glasses more often.

Dear God,
As I make my way to the manger, help me to see others as You do.

Lisa M. Black

Trading Plans

Because Joseph her husband was faithful to the law, and yet did not want to expose her to public disgrace, he had in mind to divorce her quietly. But after he had considered this, an angel of the Lord appeared to him in a dream and said, "Joseph son of David, do not be afraid to take Mary home as your wife, because what is conceived in her is from the Holy Spirit."
—Matthew 1:19–20 NIV

"For I know the plans I have for you," declares the LORD, "plans to prosper you and not to harm you, plans to give you hope and a future."
—Jeremiah 29:11 NIV

Joseph had figured out his path, and it did not include a pregnant fiancée. His plan was faithful to the law and kind under the circumstances. Of course, God's response to Joseph's plan was "Not so fast, Joseph. I have another way planned for you." God's plan required Joseph to rely on Him daily and make a big leap of faith.

Our ways are not God's ways. God's plan is to give us hope and a future—a long-range future and not just the future of this life. In making our way to the manger, we know the goal, but we don't know God's plan for getting us there. There is no God Google Maps app that tells us where God wants us to turn and how much farther we must go before we get to our destination. We seem to get directions on a need-to-know basis.

The message of the manger is God's plan of hope and a future. When the angel said to Joseph, "Do not be afraid of the completely different plan that I have for you," the angel could be saying that to each one of us as well. It's not easy to discern God's plan for us. Sometimes it seems impossible. That's when faith in God and hope for the future are the only maps we have.

In accepting God's plan and abandoning his own, Joseph took a challenging path—one filled with ridicule, embarrassment, and humiliation. In return, he got to be the earthly father of Jesus. Joseph got to spend each day with Jesus, teach Him his trade of carpentry, help mold the man Jesus would be, watch Jesus grow, cradle Him in his arms, and love Him as his own son. Joseph got a great deal all because he was willing to trust that God had a plan for him. Joseph prospered not financially but spiritually. He trusted in God's plan for the future and got to be Jesus's dad in exchange. How cool is that?

Dear God,
Just for today, let's trade plans—I'll take
Yours and walk in faith and hope.

Clouds Are Good

In those days Mary set out and went with haste to a
Judean town in the hill country, where she entered
the house of Zechariah and greeted Elizabeth.
—Luke 1:39–40 NRSV

Therefore, since we are surrounded by so great a
cloud of witnesses, let us also lay aside every weight
and the sin which clings so closely, and let us run
with perseverance the race that is set before us.
—Hebrews 12:1 ESV

On day 8, I mentioned how we don't make our way to the manger
alone—that we have people who have helped us along the way
and we, in turn, help others on their way to the manger. Mary had
two godly people to help her along the way, two people who, more
than anyone else, would understand the miracle she had received.
Other people most certainly would have thought Mary was crazy
announcing that she was pregnant with the Son of God, but Zechariah
and Elizabeth were totally on board with God's plan. It is such a gift
to be able to go to someone who understands you. For Mary, that
person was Elizabeth. Agreeing to be the mother of the Son of God,
while a tremendous honor, must have also been frightening and a
huge weight for a young girl to bear. With Elizabeth, Mary could set
aside that weight, have a respite, and gear up for the race that was
set before her.

Those of us who belong to a community of faith, or who were raised in families where faith was important, are surrounded by a cloud of witnesses—people who have supported and encouraged us along our way. I was blessed to grow up in a church in Yakima, Washington, with people who supported and nurtured the youth of the church through their financial contributions, taught Sunday school, served as youth leaders, and prayed for me over the years. They were my cloud of witnesses from very early on. I have since been a member of another church that has supported and nurtured me and my family for many years.

Take a moment today to thank God for your cloud of witnesses, the people who have walked with you on your way to the manger, the people who have encouraged you and supported you in your faith. We all carry extra weight (stress, anger, grief, fear, etc.) and sin, but remembering your cloud of witnesses may help lift that weight when you realize how much you are loved and have been loved. So, to my cloud of witnesses, thank you—I am blessed because of you.

Dear God,
Thank You for the cloud of witnesses who surround me both here and in heaven and for the ways they have helped form my faith.

God Is Greater

They [the frogs from the second plague] were piled into heaps, and the land reeked of them. But when Pharaoh saw that there was relief, he hardened his heart and would not listen to Moses and Aaron, just as the LORD had said.
—Exodus 8:14–15 NIV

When Herod realized that he had been outwitted by the Magi, he was furious, and he gave orders to kill all the boys in Bethlehem and its vicinity who were two years old and under, in accordance with the time he had learned from the Magi.
—Matthew 2:16 NIV

King Herod and Pharaoh had much in common. Pharaoh's hardened heart ultimately resulted in the tenth and most deadly plague before the Hebrews were released from Egypt. Herod's hard heart and fear likewise led to the killing of untold numbers of children. How does this apply to our way to the manger?

Moses and the Hebrews maintained their focus on their goal despite the immense power and opposition of Pharaoh. The wise men were strangers in a strange land, also subject to the power of Herod and Rome, and yet they, too, stayed on their path—they found the infant king and a way around Herod. Herod and Pharaoh were no match for the plans God laid to save His people.

When we are faced with those who would seek to prevent God's plans from coming to fruition, or seek to prevent us from making our way to the manger, it's good to remember that God is greater. Unexpected detours may impact our way to the manger, but they can also be elements of change and growth. When our way to the manger seems to be completely off the rails, we need to remember the paths that others took—the stories of faith and heroism during World War II and of cancer victims who lived their lives with hope and bravely endured experimental treatments for the benefit of those who follow them are just two examples. Detours on our way to the manger may result in our learning more, risking more, and growing more than we could have imagined. When I'm faced with a hardened heart, maybe my response should be to be willing to take another path, like the wise men—a path I had not considered that will still get me where I want to be.

Dear God,
Give me courage in all circumstances to
continue on my way to the manger.

What's Your Perspective?

> Every valley shall be exalted, and every mountain
> and hill shall be made low: and the crooked shall
> be made straight, and the rough places plain.
> —Isaiah 40:4 KJB

> In those days came John the Baptist, preaching in the wilderness
> of Judaea, and saying, Repent ye: for the kingdom of heaven
> is at hand. For this is he that was spoken of by the prophet
> [Isaiah], saying, The voice of one crying in the wilderness,
> Prepare ye the way of the Lord, make his paths straight.
> —Matthew 3:1–3 KJB

Our Christmas tree is crooked. We put it up last weekend, and I noticed the other day that it's crooked. Not Leaning Tower of Pisa crooked, but it's crooked. When we put the tree up, my husband held the tree, and I looked at it and then secured the trunk in the base. At the time, it seemed to be perfectly straight, but I don't think I looked at the tree from enough angles.

I have read the verse from Matthew from the same angle for many, many years, but today, for the first time, I saw something I had not seen before: the words in Matthew are not exactly the same as the words in Isaiah. In Isaiah, it says that "the crooked shall *be made* straight," but in Matthew, it's "*make* his paths straight." Isaiah implies that what is crooked will be made straight by someone, but in Matthew, John the Baptist was telling his listeners to "make his paths straight." There's a big difference, to my way of thinking. Is God making the path straight, or is that supposed to be my job? Or is it supposed to be a combination of the two?

Clearly what seems straight to me at one point or from one angle is not straight from another—case in point, our Christmas tree. How is it that from one point of view something seems so obviously right but from another point of view wildly crooked? I see on a regular basis how people firmly believe that their position is the right and fair one, but those positions don't always align, usually because people are looking at the situation from different perspectives.

God sees all perspectives. He knows how to make the path straight. Jesus's birth was the fulfillment of God's plan back in Genesis. From Genesis to Matthew and Luke, the way to the manger was clear, even though it seems wonky to us. God used every single circumstance to get His people one step closer to the manger.

As we anticipate Jesus coming again, we can't see the way because it's really wonky—with wars and conflict on so many levels, nothing looks even close to being prepared for His coming. From my perspective, things look crooked, but from God's perspective, things are heading straight to His coming. I still don't know who's making the path straight, but I know that God's path is the right one and I need to get my path aligned with His.

Dear God,
Help me line my perspective up with Yours
as I make my way to the manger.

Lisa M. Black

DAY 15

Joyful, Joyous, Joy!

Shout aloud and sing for joy, people of Zion, for
great is the Holy One of Israel among you.
—Isaiah 12:6 NIV

But the angel said to them, "Do not be afraid. I bring you
good news that will cause great joy for all the people."
—Luke 2:10 NIV

My girlfriend and her mom came to New Jersey to visit a while back. My girlfriend had not been to New Jersey in more than twenty years, and her mom had never been here, so we had a terrific time doing touristy things. It was all great and fun, but the highlight of all the New York events for my girlfriend's mom was seeing a Broadway show. When we left the theater, we grabbed abandoned playbills off the floor so she could take them back home and give them to her friends. We must have walked out of the theater with about a dozen playbills. When my girlfriend's mom got back home, she was so excited to share those playbills and talk about her New York experience. It was equally delightful to see her so full of joy!

Like the shepherds with their encounter with the angels in the field, seeing something new and huge is overwhelming. Why the shepherds didn't just drop to the ground and pass out is beyond me. It's a good thing I wasn't a shepherd—it would have been a much shorter story and would have included a line about an angel splashing water on my face.

How do you respond when you experience something exciting? Do you keep it to yourself, or do you call your family and friends and post it on social media? Based on what I see on social media, if people can get excited about what they're eating, they should be at least that excited about the birth of Jesus. Let's face it: the birth of Jesus is a bigger event than the heart-shaped blueberry pancake you made for breakfast.

I don't think God expects us to stand on a street corner yelling about the birth of Christ, but I do think He expects us to show some excitement about it—some *joy* about it. Every so often, we should shout aloud and sing for joy, for great is the Holy One among us. I know it's hard for people to raise their hands and dance when singing praise songs in church—I get that—but you'd better be raising your hands and dancing up a storm in your heart, at least occasionally! Great is the Holy One among us. Emmanuel. God with us.

How will you express your joy this Advent season? Will you sing more loudly in church (or at least in your car)? Will you be kinder to strangers? Contribute to those in need? Share your faith and spread the joy? What are you going to do? You need to share the joy!

Dear God,
Fill me with Your good news so that I can share the joy!

"A Way to the Manger"

For he will command his angels concerning
you to guard you in all your ways.
—Psalm 91:11 NIV

Instead of the usual format for today's devotion, a poem seemed a
good way to get today's point across.

A way to the manger
Should be so easy to see.
There's a star in the sky;
Just how hard could it be?

The child who we worship
Was announced at the start.
God wanted to save us
Though our sin broke His heart.

The prophet Isaiah
Wrote so much about Jesus—
From his birth to his death,
How he always oversees us.

The wise men were smart
And knew just what to follow.
The shepherds were simple
But brave, honest fellows.

The way planned for Mary
Was not easy at all,
But when asked to raise Jesus,
She said yes to the call.

This was certainly not
The path Joseph had planned,
But he too, responded,
And he took Mary's hand.

Our way to the manger
Is a path that's not clear,
But walking with Jesus,
We have nothing to fear.

So walk it with joy—
You don't follow a stranger.
Follow His light
On your way to the manger.

Welcome the Stranger

"At this festive season of the year, Mr. Scrooge," said the gentleman, taking up a pen, "it is more than usually desirable that we should make some slight provision for the Poor and destitute, who suffer greatly at the present time. Many thousands are in want of common necessaries; hundreds of thousands are in want of common comforts, sir."
—Charles Dickens, *A Christmas Carol*

For I was hungry and you gave me food, I was thirsty and you gave me something to drink, I was a stranger and you welcomed me.
—Matthew 25:35 ESV

We encounter all sorts of people on our way to the manger. It is very easy during Christmas to get caught up in the shopping, wrapping, baking, and merrymaking and forget about those in need. Many thousands are in want of common necessaries (a warm meal), and hundreds of thousands are in want of common comforts (a warm handshake or a kind word). Jesus was born to a poor couple. They didn't have a whole lot. Mary rode a donkey to Bethlehem, not a camel, and Joseph probably didn't have the financial ability to arrange for lodging in advance, so he and Mary were prepared to make the best of it. Jesus didn't have a soft feather bed with cashmere blankets; he was wrapped in strips of cloth and laid in a manger of hay.

Imagine Mary and Joseph in more modern times—driving into town in a beat-up, broken-down car, looking for a room at a run-down highway motel, and being told they can park their car in the garage out in the back of the property with the other junked-out cars. Imagine Jesus being born in the back seat of the car, with Mary and Joseph scared out of their minds that something might go wrong with the birth but too poor to go to the hospital. And since they're strangers in an unfamiliar town, they have no one to call to help them.

As you make your way to the manger, do you recognize Jesus in the eyes of the stranger? In the passage from Matthew, it's the last clause that strikes me the most. I can give a homeless person in New York City five dollars or a sandwich and keep walking. I can give someone a bottle of cold water on a hot summer day and go on my way. But to welcome a stranger requires a bigger commitment: it requires a connection. You don't get to just walk away; you have to stay, you have to make eye contact, and you have to recognize that person has value and is a child of God. *That* is what it means to welcome a stranger.

We can't make our way to the manger with tunnel vision because if we do, we miss the opportunity to encounter Jesus and we miss the opportunity to actually do something for Him. Considering how much time we spend asking Him for stuff, shouldn't we welcome opportunities to do something for Him?

Dear God,
Open my eyes to the opportunities to serve
You on my way to the manger.

Devotion Writing 101

But he said to me, "My grace is sufficient for you, for my power is made perfect in weakness." Therefore I will boast all the more gladly about my weaknesses, so that Christ's power may rest on me.
—2 Corinthians 12:9 NIV

What follows is one of my daily internal dialogues with God:

Lisa: God, I don't know what to write today.

God: I know. You usually don't. That's why I'm here to help you.

Lisa: Nothing interesting happened to me today—nothing funny, nothing poignant. I went to work, and that was it. To be frank, I got nothin'.

God: Your name is Lisa, not Frank.

Lisa: You're hilarious, God. Now can we get serious? I have a devotion to write!

God: Open your Bible.

Lisa: I have been through the story of Jesus's birth a hundred times, maybe a thousand! What is left to write that will have any meaning to anyone? Can't I just point to You and say, "Go"?

God: Open your Bible.

Lisa: Ugh. OK. Is there something in here about Mary and Joseph stopping at a rest stop? I could write a devotion about being tired and needing a day off.

God: That's not where we're going with this.

Lisa (*in a whiny voice*): But I can't write one today.

God: On your way to the manger, you will get tired, you will feel defeated, you may even want to turn around and go back to where you came from, but I have a bigger plan. My grace is sufficient for you, for My power is made perfect in weakness. That's 2 Corinthians 12:9, in case you were wondering.

Lisa: I love that verse.

God: I know. I love that verse too. My grace is sufficient for you, even—no, *especially*—when you got nothin'.

Lisa: OK, God, give me Your words because I don't have any. Shine Your light on my darkness and show me what You want me to say. Make Your power perfect in my weakness, because I am *really* weak. Bring it, God, and let's get to work. Amen.

And then we write a devotion.

Keep the Pride on the Side

When Joseph awoke from sleep, he did as the angel of
the Lord commanded him; he took her as his wife.
—Matthew 1:24 NRSV

When Herod saw that he had been tricked by the wise men,
he was infuriated, and he sent and killed all the children in
and around Bethlehem who were two years old or under.
—Matthew 2:16 NRSV

Joseph and Herod were both faced with circumstances that bruised their egos and wounded their pride. Joseph learned that his fiancée was pregnant and the child was not his. Herod learned through the wise men that a child was born in his county who was to become the king of the Jews. Both men were understandably upset. Mary's story of an immaculate conception was humiliating for Joseph—what person alive had ever heard of a woman carrying a child who was conceived by God? Even now, if a young girl were to say she was carrying a child conceived by the Holy Spirit, people would roll their eyes, smirk, and say, "Yeah, right." As for Herod, he was in a position of power over a country with many Jews, and he found out that a baby was born who was to be their king. Herod seems like a wildly insecure person. He was likely appointed by the Roman senate, and the Roman Empire was full of backstabbing political climbers. If this baby was going to be king of the Jews, then what would Herod's role be? Who would he rule over? Like Joseph, he was going to be humiliated.

One of our big stumbling blocks on the way to the manger is our pride. My husband and I were discussing how people often don't give money to the homeless on the street because it might be a scam and no one wants to be scammed and taken for a fool. But isn't it better to err on the side of compassion? So what if you're out five dollars? Wouldn't you rather stand before God and say, "I foolishly gave money to someone who lied to me" rather than "I foolishly refused to give money to someone who needed it"? I know which side of that equation I would rather be on, even if I don't always do it. God doesn't want us to be fools, but He also wants us to be compassionate—it isn't easy.

Joseph and Herod were faced with circumstances that challenged their pride: a pregnant fiancée and a worthless throne. Herod unleashed a horrible response—because of his pride, he murdered untold numbers of children, and he still didn't get the child he was after. He lived a dissatisfied, insecure, soulless existence. Joseph, on the other hand, put aside his pride, married Mary, was father to Jesus, and was secure in the knowledge that he had been obedient to God. Herod's way to the manger was blocked by his pride, but Joseph put aside his pride and made his way to the manger walking side by side with Jesus (literally).

How is pride impacting your way to the manger?

Dear God,
Give me the strength to not let my pride
block my way to the manger.

An Interesting Family Tree

Judah the father of Perez and Zerah by Tamar … and Salmon
the father of Boaz by Rahab, and Boaz the father of Obed by
Ruth … And David was the father of Solomon by the wife of
Uriah … and Jacob the father of Joseph the husband of Mary.
—Matthew 1:1–17 NRSV

When Jesus heard this, he said to them, "Those who are
well have no need of a physician, but those who are sick;
I have come to call not the righteous but sinners."
—Mark 2:17 NRSV

Jesus had a very interesting family tree. The women identified in his
genealogy included Tamar, who was treated horribly by her in-laws
and got pregnant by tricking Judah; Rahab, who was a prostitute;
Ruth, a widow in a foreign land; "the wife of Uriah," Bathsheba, who
committed adultery (but then so did David); and Mary, a young girl
who got pregnant before she got married. Funny, I don't see Mother
Teresa, Elizabeth I, or Madame Curie types on the list, but to be
honest, I'm glad I don't. The men on the list aren't all that fabulous
either: Jacob ripped off his brother Esau for his birthright; Boaz made
Ruth sleep on the floor; David was an adulterer, murderer, and pretty
poor father; Solomon was wise but turned out to be a hot mess;
Rehoboam was a bad king (Israel split under his leadership); and
Hezekiah was a bad king too. My point is that Jesus's earthly lineage
was full of sinful people but He was without sin.

If you are reading these devotions, you're probably trying to make your way to the manger this Advent season, but where you started and how far along you have gotten are as unique as you are. You may have a long history of being a believer and just need a little daily encouragement. Maybe you fell off the path a while ago and are trying to get back on track. Maybe you only read these devotions after you've finished playing solitaire on your phone. Our path to the manger is a rocky one, filled with all kinds of sin along the way, but Jesus knows that—the stories of His earthly family were enough to fill a book, the Old Testament in fact. Jesus's genealogy tells us that He was well acquainted with the ways that we mess up but He came to save us anyway. There's nothing in your life or your past that would shock Him. He's calling us—the sinners, the breakers of the Ten Commandments, the selfish, the foolish, the power hungry, the prideful. He came for us. Not only does He want us to make our way to the manger, but He's also eager to walk with us and find us other people to walk with. We are not all compassionate like Mother Teresa, strong leaders like Elizabeth I, or intelligent like Madame Curie, but we are worth it to God. You are worth it!

Dear God,
When I'm overwhelmed with feeling like I'm not
good enough, remind me that You came to save
me and help me on my way to the manger.

Quiet Words and Silent Night

The quiet words of the wise are more to be heeded
than the shouting of a ruler among fools.
—Ecclesiastes 9:17 NRSV

On entering the house, they saw the child with Mary
his mother; and they knelt down and paid him homage.
Then, opening their treasure chests, they offered
him gifts of gold, frankincense, and myrrh.
—Matthew 2:11 NRSV

Imagine the scene of the wise men entering the house where Jesus was with Mary. I think it's interesting that this description doesn't indicate what words were exchanged between the wise men and Mary, but I get a sense that there weren't a lot of words spoken. Some experiences are too great for words; some sights demand quiet and reverence. Spectacular sunrises and sunsets, a shooting star, great cathedrals, a newborn in your arms, and imagined but unexpected victories are just a few examples of the power of silence—times when you just soak it in because you just don't have the words to describe what you're experiencing. The wise men came before the child they recognized as a king, knelt, and offered Him their gifts, and then they went home. There was no big public announcement, no press release, no fanfare—just some quiet words with Mary and Joseph, and then the wise men went on their way.

The gift of quiet words is not one I open very often. The gift of *blathering on* is one I open regularly, so I appreciate those who make an impact with their quiet words. There's not a lot of quiet during Advent. There's a lot of music, traffic and commotion in stores, and activity, so much so that it's hard to find a quiet moment to just reflect with awe on the magnitude of Jesus's birth. I think that's why I like the song "Silent Night." I like the scene in *A Charlie Brown Christmas* when all the kids are quiet in the auditorium and Linus steps up the microphone and recites Luke 2. I like Christmas morning when the house is still before all the unwrapping, cooking, and gathering with family starts.

We are a week away from Christmas, and it will be a busy week, but the way to the manger needs to include some quiet words, some quiet time to reflect on Jesus's birth. Finding quiet time is hard—maybe you need to actually schedule it—but try to do it. Jesus entered this world as an infant. He couldn't speak. He could only cry and coo like babies do. The quiet words of Jesus, his quiet presence, are more to be heeded than all the rest. Quiet is not my strength, but I know that it's only in the quiet moments that I can hear God speak. It's only in the quiet that I can rest in Him. It's in the quiet that I can honestly and sincerely offer to Him the gifts I have. Find your quiet during this last week of Advent. Enjoy some quiet time on your way to the manger. It will restore your soul.

Dear God,
As I make my way to the manger, quiet my
spirit so that I may worship You.

FOURTH SUNDAY OF ADVENT
The Way of Love

For God so loved the world that he gave his only
Son, so that everyone who believes in him may
not perish but may have eternal life.
—John 3:16 NRSV

But the angel said to them, "Do not be afraid; for
see—I am bringing you good news of great joy for
all the people: to you is born this day in the city of
David a Savior, who is the Messiah, the Lord."
—Luke 2:10–11 NRSV

The fourth Sunday of Advent is the Sunday of love, and there is a
lot of love in the story of Jesus's birth: the love between Mary and
Joseph, the love between Mary and her cousin, Elizabeth; and the
love that Mary had for God as evidenced by her obedience to his call.
The greatest love, though, is the love that God demonstrated for the
world in giving us His only Son.

I would not presume to explain the mystery of the Trinity. I have
only a simple understanding, but I know that it is far greater than
what I can comprehend. If we accept that the Father, Son, and Holy
Spirit are three distinct yet united entities, then we realize God kind
of became an empty nester when he sent His only Son to earth. I
know that God and Jesus stayed in regular contact, and I know that
they were one, but Jesus was God in human form, and they were in

two different places, heaven and earth. John 3:16 says that God gave His Son, so there was some aspect of relinquishment on God's part.

Two of my most difficult days were the days that each of my children left for college. I was thrilled that they were off to start such wonderful adventures, but that didn't stop me from doing the big ugly cry when I walked out of their dorm rooms. As happy as I was for them, my heart was broken; I felt like part of me was missing. Sending Jesus to earth to save us was God's plan from the start. Jesus's death was Jesus's sacrifice for us, but Jesus's birth was a sacrifice for God too—He sacrificed, for a time, the communion they shared. Jesus faced ridicule from the time he was born, He was in danger from the start because of Herod, and then He faced many challenges during His ministry, not to mention His death on the cross. There were wonderful moments, but there were also a lot of horrible moments and experiences. I can't comprehend the depth of love that it took for God to allow His only Son to go through all of that. But it He did it: He gave his only Son so that whoever believes in Him could have eternal life.

The way to the manger is paved with love. Love is the beginning, love is what sustains us, and love is what saves us. Love is the good news of great joy and is the reason why we have hope for the future. A way to the manger always includes love.

Dear God,
Your love for me is greater than I can comprehend, and it came at a great price. It is good news of great joy—don't let me forget it.

DAY
23

Footprints in the Snow

I will lead the blind by a road they do not know, by paths they
have not known I will guide them. I will turn the darkness
before them into light, the rough places into level ground.
These are the things I will do, and I will not forsake them.
—Isaiah 42:16 NRSV

But he knows the way that I take; when he has
tested me, I shall come out like gold.
—Job 23:10 NRSV

We had just enough snow the other day to see the footprints of our
dog and of the bunnies who live in our garage in our backyard. There
was no rhyme or reason to their paths—they crisscrossed, made
sharp turns, stopped, retraced steps, and seemed to go absolutely
nowhere. As I looked out the window over the backyard, I thought,
That's what my way to the manger looks like. I've always liked the
"Footsteps" poem about the footsteps in the sand, but looking at the
crazy patchwork of steps in the snow, I realized that my way to the
manger looks a lot more like that than the steady forward progress
of the path in the sand.

My way to the manger seems to include a lot of going back over
ground that I've covered before. Just when I think I have one area
dedicated to God or am no longer struggling with something that's
impeding my way to the manger, I end up retracing my steps and

struggling with the same thing or something similar again. It would be so great to say, "I've conquered the whole impatience thing; now I'm a very patient person"; check off the box; and not have to deal with it again, but that's not how it works, at least not for me. Sometimes my victory over something lasts a day, maybe two, and then I'm right back where I started. It could be an old hurt that I think I've overcome, but then it comes up in conversation, and I struggle with it all over again. I might as well be a bunny in the snow—my way to the manger looks just the same.

Isaiah tells us that God takes us on roads and paths that we don't know but that He will guide us, bring light to the darkness, and level the rough places. The last sentence is my favorite: "These are the things I *will* do, and I will *not forsake* them." God knows that my path looks as chaotic as a bunny path in the snow, but when He brings me through it, I will come out like gold. I have to let God lead me on paths that are unfamiliar and put my trust in Him. If I can do that, God will not forsake me. He won't leave me to fend for myself. He will use my way to the manger to refine me, to sift out the stuff I don't need, so that what's left is the gold. God will guide me when I'm in unfamiliar territory. God will light my way when it's dark and frightening. God will smooth the rough places so that my foot will not falter. He knows where I'm going, so even when it looks like bunny and dog tracks in the snow, He sees the bigger picture, and I am not alone on my way to the manger.

Dear God,
Thank You for knowing my way to the manger,
even when I do not.

Have You Seen a King around Here?

> In the time of King Herod, after Jesus was born in Bethlehem
> of Judea, wise men from the East came to Jerusalem, asking,
> "Where is the child who has been born king of the Jews? For we
> observed his star at its rising, and have come to pay him homage."
> —Matthew 2:1–2 NRSV

> When they had heard the king, they set out; and there,
> ahead of them, went the star that they had seen at its rising,
> until it stopped over the place where the child was.
> —Matthew 2:9 NRSV

The star in the story of Jesus's birth is more than a prop—it's a character. The wise men from the east followed it as far as Jerusalem and checked in with the local authorities to see whether anyone there had noticed this remarkable star. I get the sense that the wise men kind of lost track of the star for a while because they stopped and asked for directions. The wise men believed that the people who lived in the area would have noticed the star and put the pieces together. However, Herod obviously had no clue, so he called together his advisers. The advisers didn't seem to know anything about a star either, but they knew the prophecy about where the Messiah was to be born. After the wise men left Herod, "there, ahead of them, went the star"—they were able to pick up the scent again, and the star led them right to the place where Jesus was.

Lisa M. Black

Our way to manger can be a lot like the wise men's journey to Jesus. When we first believe, we get a glimpse of the star, or the light of God, and have that period of clarity when we know where we want to go. We enthusiastically start on our way to the manger, but then we can lose sight of the light, take our eyes off God, make our own path, and get lost. Eventually, if we're wise, we stop and ask for directions.

It took the wise men approximately two years from the time they saw the star to the time they found Jesus. I don't know how far they traveled, but two years is a long time. I get bored and antsy on a five-hour flight to Seattle. It had to be a trip of faith because they could see the star only at night, or not at all, if it was cloudy. I'm sure they were traveling with a certain degree of haste, just in case the star disappeared as quickly as it presented itself. Our light won't burn out, but there are times when we lose sight of it.

Have you experienced times when you just couldn't see the star ahead of you? Times when the clouds are so thick that you lose your way? We need to follow the example of the wise men: when we lose our way, we need to stop and get help. Get some encouragement and guidance from the Bible or a friend, and then that clarity you had at the beginning can reemerge, and you can get to the place where Jesus is.

Dear God,
When I lose sight of Your light, please direct
me so I can get back on my way.

Listen

In the sixth month of Elizabeth's pregnancy, God sent the
angel Gabriel to Nazareth, a town in Galilee, to a virgin
pledged to be married to a man named Joseph, a descendant
of David. The virgin's name was Mary. The angel went to
her and said, "Greetings, you who are highly favored! The
Lord is with you." Mary was greatly troubled at his words
and wondered what kind of greeting this might be.
—Luke 1:26–29 NIV

My sheep listen to my voice; I know them, and they follow me.
—John 10:27 NIV

When you read this passage of Gabriel's encounter with Mary, don't
you wonder why Mary was "greatly troubled" and "wondered what
kind of greeting this might be"? His words were straightforward and
actually really great: Mary was highly favored, and the Lord was
with her. Mary's reaction is common for a lot of us on our way to the
manger. We don't always recognize God's messages to us because we
either are unfamiliar with His voice or don't want to listen to Him.
Let's face it: we are cynical and more likely to question the motives
of the speaker than to embrace the message.

The first option—not recognizing God's voice—is usually the result
of not being in the habit of listening to Him. There are some voices
that you would recognize in an instant because you've heard them so

often. The voices of your parents or your children are recognizable. Darth Vader, for example, has a very recognizable voice and breathing pattern. Linus reading the story of Jesus's birth is another recognizable voice. It's a matter of exposure. The more you listen to God's voice, the more obvious it is when you hear it. That doesn't necessarily mean you will do what He says, but you will know where the message is coming from.

The second option—refusing to believe it's God speaking to you and choosing to not listen—is more dangerous. That's when we become like Herod and Pharaoh and we harden our hearts against God. We are skeptical of His power and of His love. It's more than just doubting; it's rejecting Him. It's about letting our pride prevent us from taking a risk, from stepping out in faith.

Mary didn't understand the greeting, and she may not have immediately known God was speaking to her through the angel, but she listened. God knew her, and Mary followed. Like Mary, we may not recognize God's voice right away, but we need to have hearts that are open so that we *can* hear His voice. God talks to us, directs us, and encourages us as we are on our way to the manger. We need ears to hear, and that comes from having open hearts—hearts free of pride, skepticism, and fear. How can you recognize His voice if you never listen?

Dear God,
Give me ears to hear so that I will recognize
Your voice when You call.

Pray First

Do not be anxious about anything, but in every situation, by prayer and petition, with thanksgiving, present your requests to God. And the peace of God, which transcends all understanding, will guard your hearts and your minds in Christ Jesus.
—Philippians 4:6–7 NIV

The day our son, Nicholas, proposed to his girlfriend, Holly, was wonderful, and it provided God with a teaching opportunity for me. Nicholas planned to surprise Holly and propose to her with family and friends secretly watching. The timing for all of this was crucial because (1) my husband and I had to drive three hours to Pennsylvania to be there at 12:30 p.m. to see it all happen and (2) I had to be back in New Jersey by 3:30 p.m. to perform in a 4:00 p.m. matinee of *A Christmas Carol*. It was a lot of driving with a lot left to chance. My husband and I took separate cars so that he could stay for the party while I came back to New Jersey. The weather and the traffic were awful that morning, and it seemed to take forever to get out of New Jersey. So, of course, being the strong, devotion-writing person I am, I did exactly what you would expect: I worried, cried, and called my husband, blubbering into the phone that I was never going to make it—I wasn't going to see Nicholas propose, as I'd have to turn around and come back to New Jersey, missing this moment that our son had invited us to attend.

It was only *after* I talked to my husband and finished crying that I thought it would be a good idea to pray about it. (My next devotion series will be about praying first to avoid flipping out.) As I was driving through the snow, rain, and traffic, I prayed and remembered that my way had already been laid out. If it was God's plan that I make it to see the proposal, I would make it, so crying and worrying were not going to change a thing. If it was not God's plan for me to be there, there would be another way figured out and it would be OK.

The plan was for me to be there, because we arrived in time, I saw Nicholas propose, I saw Holly say yes, and it was wonderful. I also got back to New Jersey in time to go onstage for the 4:00 p.m. performance of the show, and everything was just fine.

Our way to the manger is filled with all kinds of anxiety: Are we going the right way? What if something doesn't go according to "our plan"? What if our way is blocked by circumstances beyond our control? What if, what if, what if. This is a lesson that God has to teach me repeatedly: "Do not be anxious about anything," and instead pray about it. I could have what if'd myself silly, but it wasn't until I prayed and just allowed God to work it out that my anxiety level dropped and I just kept driving, trusting in God along the way. Prayer is God's peace on my way to the manger.

Dear God,
When I am anxious and worried, let my first act be to pray.

It's Been a Winding Path

"For I know the plans I have for you," declares
the LORD, "plans to prosper you and not to harm
you, plans to give you hope and a future."
—Jeremiah 29:11 NIV

Our way to the manger has been quite a trip. Like most trips, it meandered through different topics—life generally doesn't lend itself to topic-specific chapters that we resolve before we go on to the next challenge. It started at a raspberry bush, then continued on to the Garden of Eden, to see where God's way to the manger began. We saw how Moses and the Hebrews took their circuitous route to the Promised Land as they got Egypt and four hundred years of slavery out of their systems. Then we had a brief stop for some Parker House rolls and saw how messy our way to the manger can be. Zechariah reminded us of the importance of trusting God, and in a weird way, Darth Vader brought us some joy. As we looked at Bethlehem, we were reminded of the magnitude of God's plan. We then were reminded that we are responsible to reflect the light of God so that others can find their way to the manger—that we need to see others through God glasses and remember that God's plan is one of hope for the future for all who believe in Him.

We don't make our way to the manger alone; we have a cloud of witnesses who have gone before us and travel with us. We also face detours that take us off the way we think we should go, but since God never loses track of us, we can still make our way to the manger. My crooked Christmas tree was next up and served to remind us that, although things seem so wonky, God uses all circumstances to bring us to Him. We can't get through Advent without joy, so get excited! The recap poem gave us a break. The devotion about the stranger / the homeless and how pride can prevent us from extending a helping hand challenged us to live what we believe all year long. Then there was the conversation devotion about relying on God when we got nothin'. Pride versus compassion was the topic in the next devotion: we must be willing to help the stranger, because in doing that, we are helping Jesus.

Jesus's family tree should serve to remind us that Jesus is well acquainted with sinners and came for us anyway. During this busy season, we all need a moment of quiet so that we can hear His voice and be reminded of His great love and sacrifice in giving us His only Son. The bunny tracks in the snow served as another visual reminder of how our path to the manger can seem so confused and yet God is with us, guiding us. The star over Bethlehem was God's guide to the wise men, but when it wasn't visible, stopping and asking for directions was important. It's also important to get into the habit of listening for God—the more we listen, the easier it is to recognize His voice. And, of course, we don't get far on our way to the manger without prayer. See how far we've come this Advent season?

Dear God,
The way may seem unfamiliar or difficult, but thank
You for being with me on my way to the manger.

A Christmas Poem

While they were there, the time came for the baby to be born, and she gave birth to her firstborn, a son. She wrapped him in cloths and placed him in a manger, because there was no guest room available for them.
—Luke 2:6–7 NIV

"'Twas the Night before Christ's Birth"

'Twas the night before Christ's birth, when all through the stable
The creatures were restless—they didn't have cable.
The hay was a mess, strewn about without care.
The night air was frigid—not a soul would be there.

The inn guests were nestled all snug in their beds,
While Mary and Joseph sought cover for their heads.
The innkeeper was busy, when he heard the loud tap.
"There's no room in here. Go sleep out in back."

So off to the cave, which was dark, cold, and dry,
Went the tired young couple to pass the night by.
They prepared for the coming of their new baby boy,
The child who would come to bring so much joy.

The stars shone so bright on the pasture below.
The shepherds were basking in the warmth of the glow,
When what to their wondering eyes did appear
But a sky full of angels, and their song they did hear.

The angels sang tidings of great joy and good news.
For all who would listen, it was hope they could use.
More brilliant than starlight the angels did shine.
They sang of a savior who would come to be mine.

"You'll find the dear child in a manger of hay!
Now go see the baby before the dawn of the day.
In the stable with Mary and Joseph you'll find him.
Go. Leave these sheep. Don't worry—we'll mind them."

The streets were so dark as the men made their way.
Are angels for real? Do they mean what they say?
A baby was born who would save all mankind?
Where was this baby? Who would they find?

In a land far away lived three kings who had seen
A remarkable star—in the heavens it gleamed.
Their books prophesied about a great king,
So they saddled their camels; who could miss such a thing?

They readied their gifts to present to the child,
But what does one give to one so meek and so mild?
Gold for a king would acknowledge his power,
And myrrh would be used in his most desperate hour.

The last gift of frankincense was so costly and smelly.
Maybe instead of perfume, he would like food for his belly.
They traveled for days with their eyes on the star.
The road led to Bethlehem they had traveled so far.

Jesus was sleeping in a small wooden manger.
Mary and Joseph were keeping watch for all danger.
The wise men and shepherds took them both by surprise.
They couldn't help but take note of the joy in their eyes.

These people had come to worship their son,
The child of the Most Holy, the Glorious One.
They accepted the gifts and the words of high praise
And remembered the night for the rest of their days.

The shepherds rejoiced as they went back to their sheep.
The wise men were warned by a dream in their sleep.
The world didn't know that its Savior was born,
A healer for all whose lives had been torn.

The angels kept singing their song in the night,
Shouting out to the world that all would be right.
"Glory to God in the highest!" they sang strong and true.
"Goodwill toward all people, and God's peace to you!"

Merry Christmas!

CHRISTMAS DAY
Active Waiting

> For God so loved the world that he gave his only
> Son, so that everyone who believes in him may
> not perish but may have eternal life.
> —John 3:16 NRSV

Merry Christmas! Advent is over, and we celebrate the birth of Christ today. Light your white Christ candle on your Advent wreath, if you have one. The anticipation of Christ's birth is over, but the anticipation of His coming again continues. Our way to the manger won't really end until we see Him again.

I think John 3:16 is such a well-known verse and one of the first verses we memorize because it really is the most basic thing we need to know about God: We worship a God who wants to be in relationship with us. We worship a God who sacrificed the most precious thing to save us. We worship a God who wants to spend eternity with us. Considering there are some people I'm not sure I'd want to spend five minutes with, that's saying a lot.

May God bless you with peace when you're anxious, encouragement when you're feeling *ugh*, love when you're feeling worthless, and strength in your weakness. Keep making your way to the manger knowing that it is *your* way. We all take different paths, face different hurdles, and experience different victories. There is no right way and no wrong way. Our goal is the same, so stay focused. Look for God in the times things are a hot mess, and wear your God glasses to see Him in the world around you. Listen for His voice—He is speaking to you, so listen! Find the humor in your circumstances, and remember that even when you're unhappy you can still feel *joy*.

Merry Christmas to you and your families. Thank you for sharing these devotions with me.

Dear God,
Thank You for the gift of Your Son. Please help me
to experience Him in a new way each day.

Printed in the USA
CPSIA information can be obtained
at www.ICGtesting.com
CBHW031941221023
1445CB00002B/10